The Technology of Farming

Producing
Meat

Rachel Lynette

Chicago, Illinois

www.capstonepub.com
Visit our website to find out
more information about
Heinemann-Raintree books.

To order:

☏ Phone 888-454-2279

🖱 Visit www.capstonepub.com
to browse our catalog and order online.

© 2013 Heinemann Library
an imprint of Capstone Global Library, LLC
Chicago, Illinois

Edited by Abby Colich, Megan Cotugno, and Nancy Dickmann
Designed by Victoria Allen
Picture research by Elizabeth Alexander
Illustrations by Geoff Ward and Oxford Designers
and Illustrators

Originated by Capstone Global Library Ltd
Printed and bound in China by China Translation and Printing
Services Ltd

16 15 14 13 12
10 9 8 7 6 5 4 3 2 1

Library of Congress Cataloging-in-Publication Data
Lynette, Rachel.
  Producing meat / Rachel Lynette.—1st ed.
    p. cm.—(The technology of farming)
  Includes bibliographical references and index.
  ISBN 978-1-4329-6410-8 (hb)—ISBN 978-1-4329-6417-7 (pb)
1. Animal culture—Juvenile literature. 2. Meat—Juvenile literature. 3. Animal industry—Juvenile literature. 4. Meat industry
and trade—Juvenile literature. I. Title. II. Series: Technology of
farming.
  SF76.5.L96 2012
  664'.9—dc23
  2011037570

Acknowledgments
We would like to thank the following for permission to
reproduce photographs: Alamy: pp. 11 (© AGStockUSA), 17 (©
PhotoEdit), 21 (© SuperStock), 31 (© Felix Zaska); Corbis: pp. 8
(© Radius Images), 13 (© moodboard), 29 (© Hans Deryk/
Reuters), 30 (© Philippe Henry/First Light), 41 (© Karen
Kasmauski); Getty Images: pp. 15 (Danita Delimont/Gallo
Images), 33 (WireImage/Bennett Raglin), 34 (Samuel Aranda/
AFP), 35 (Carola Bravo/Bloomberg), 37 (Juan Mabromata/AFP),
39 (Keren Su/Stone), 43 (Mark Mawson/Robert Harding); image
courtesy of Dr Athol Klieve: p. 38; Photolibrary: p. 7 (The British
Library); Shutterstock: pp. 4 (© Martin Nemec), 12 (© LianeM),
14 (© Frontpage), 18 (© Weldon Schloneger), 22 (© Dario
Sabljak), 25 (© Phant), 26 (© Flock of sheep).

Cover photo of chicken in a pen reproduced with permission
from Getty Images (Javier Pierini/Photographer's Choice).

Every effort has been made to contact copyright holders of
any material reproduced in this book. Any omissions will
be rectified in subsequent printings if notice is given to the
publisher.

Disclaimer
All the Internet addresses (URLs) given in this book were valid
at the time of going to press. However, due to the dynamic
nature of the Internet, some addresses may have changed, or
sites may have changed or ceased to exist since publication.
While the author and publisher regret any inconvenience this
may cause readers, no responsibility for any such changes can
be accepted by either the author or the publisher.

Contents

Some words appear in the text in bold, **like this**. You can find out what they mean by looking in the glossary.

Where Does Meat Come From?

When was the last time you ate meat? Did you have bacon or sausage at breakfast or sliced turkey on your sandwich? Maybe you had a hamburger for dinner or a slice of meatloaf. Before it was on your plate, that meat was an animal that was raised on a farm.

Cows such as this one are raised for food.

Lots of livestock

The **livestock** industry is one of the largest industries on our planet. Worldwide, it feeds billions of people and employs 1.3 billion people. That means that about one in every five people on Earth work in some aspect of the livestock industry.

In the United States and many other developed countries, the majority of livestock are raised on large factory farms called **concentrated animal feeding operations**, or CAFOs. A CAFO houses large numbers of the same kind of animal in a relatively small space, usually indoors. Feeding, temperature, and waste disposal must be carefully controlled. The largest CAFOs house **poultry** and contain more than 125,000 chickens at one time!

In **developing countries**, many people still raise small herds of animals on small farms or even in their yards. In this way, families can produce meat to feed themselves as well as to sell to neighbors or at the local market. However, as these countries develop, gaining better technologies and reliable long-distance transportation, more animals are being raised on CAFOs. In most cases, it costs less money to raise an animal in a CAFO than on a farm, so once the animal is slaughtered, its meat can be sold at a lower price.

What Is the History of Meat Farming?

People began to **domesticate** animals more than 12,000 years ago in Europe, the Middle East, and Asia. They began by capturing wild animals. Then they bred them to encourage specific **traits** such as small horns, larger size, and mild **temperament**. Unlike hunting, domesticated animals provided these first farmers with a consistent food source. Many animals that we eat today, such as chickens, sheep, and pigs, were domesticated thousands of years ago.

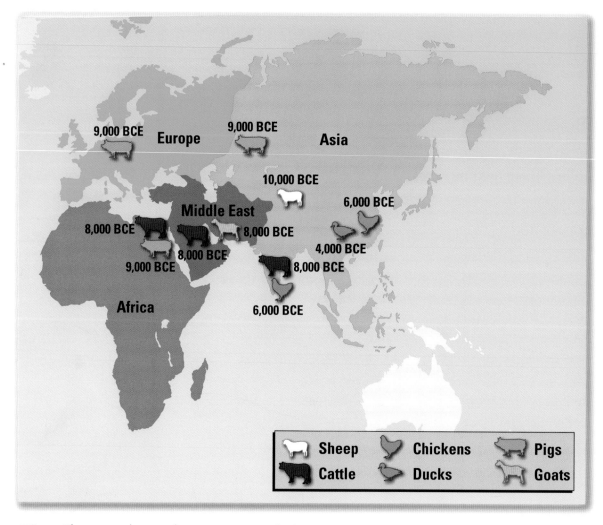

This map shows where some animals first became domesticated.

This illustration shows sheep and their farmers in the 1300s.

Feudal farming

By the sixth century CE, the **feudal system** dominated Europe. Under the feudal system, rich lords owned most of the land. The majority of the population were poor peasants or serfs who were allowed to live on the land in exchange for their labor. Although they were given small plots to farm for their own use, most of their days were spent working in the lord's fields.

A variety of animals were raised for meat during this time, including ducks, pigeons, geese, chickens, partridges, pigs, cows, and sheep. Serfs grazed their animals on common pastures. Everyone in the family helped care for the animals; however, in many cases they rarely got to eat the animals they raised. Instead the meat was taken by the lord to be used at large feasts in his manor. The feudal system deteriorated when the **bubonic plague** killed half the population of Europe in the 14th and 15th centuries and those left alive started to demand payment for their work.

Barbed Wire

Barbed wire was invented by Joseph Glidden in 1874. It revolutionized fencing for livestock, but some people felt it was cruel to the animals.

Barbed wire made it much easier for ranchers to fence in their animals.

Farming in the colonies

Before Europeans came to the Americas, American Indians had been getting most of their meat from hunting bison and other wild animals. However, they had also been raising turkeys for thousands of years. In South America, guinea pigs and alpacas were also raised for meat.

Settlers from Europe came to North and South America as well as Australia and New Zealand. They brought their **livestock** and farming methods with them. Most of the meat we eat today originally came from that livestock, many generations ago. Many European colonists started family farms and raised small flocks of chickens and other farm animals. By the 1800s, the settlers had killed most of the buffalo as well as many of the American Indians on the plains of North America. The land was used as open grazing for cattle, which were raised on large ranches. There were also many large ranches in Argentina and Brazil.

In Australia and New Zealand, settlers brought cattle, sheep, and other livestock. They took land from the **aboriginal people** who, rather than farming, had lived by hunting and gathering for thousands of years.

Mass production

In the early 1900s, advances in transportation and refrigeration made it possible to distribute meat all over the world. After World War II (1939–1945), with the introduction of fast food, there was a bigger demand for meat. In some countries small family farms gave way to larger farm operations.

How Is Beef Farmed?

The United States produces more beef than any other country. About 34 million cows are slaughtered in the United States each year. Brazil, China, India, Argentina, and Australia are also big beef producers.

The science of growing cattle

To produce inexpensive meat, farmers on large-scale factory farms must raise cattle that grow very quickly. Several technologies are used to achieve this goal. On most farms cattle spend the first part of their lives grazing on grass. However, during their last few months of life they are housed on large **feedlots** and fed a scientifically designed mix of grains so they will gain weight quickly. Cattle on feedlots gain up to 4 pounds (1.8 kilograms) per day.

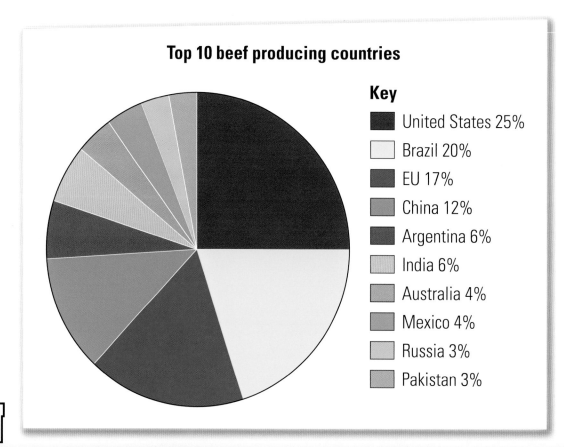

Top 10 beef producing countries

Key
- United States 25%
- Brazil 20%
- EU 17%
- China 12%
- Argentina 6%
- India 6%
- Australia 4%
- Mexico 4%
- Russia 3%
- Pakistan 3%

The grain these cattle are eating has been engineered to make them grow quickly.

This grain-rich diet combined with the crowded feedlot conditions leave the cattle vulnerable to diseases. Cattle in the U.S. are given **antibiotics** to fight these diseases. The antibiotics also promote faster growth.

In the United States, cattle are also given **growth hormones**, which not only make them grow faster but also improve the meat so that it is less fatty. However, there are concerns that meat produced using growth hormones can cause serious health problems. Because growth hormones are banned in Europe, U.S. beef cannot be sold there.

Electric Cattle Prod

Cattle farmers routinely use high-voltage electric prods to get cows to move. Although the shock is not strong enough to kill a human or cow, it is still very painful, and many people are against the use of electric cattle prods.

Sustainable beef

Sustainable farms use traditional farming methods in order to minimize harmful effects on the environment, people, and animals. Sustainable beef farms raise cattle without hormones, antibiotics, or engineered grains. Instead, small herds graze on open pastures, and their manure is used as **fertilizer**. In most cases, sustainable beef costs significantly more than beef from **CAFOs**; however, many consumers are willing to pay extra for meat that was raised **humanely** without antibiotics or growth hormones.

Sir Albert Howard
1873–1947

Born in Shropshire, England, in 1873, Albert Howard was a **botanist** and a pioneer in organic farming. When Howard was sent to India to teach the people there how to use Western farming technologies, he soon realized that he could learn more about healthy farming practices from them. He developed a method of **composting** as well as other organic farming techniques. He is the author of many important books on agriculture.

Sir Albert Howard developed a composting method that is still in use today.

Organic challenges

Sustainable beef is not necessarily **organic** beef. A farm must be certified organic in order for the beef to be labeled organic. In order to be certified, organic beef farmers must follow strict regulations, which include making sure all cattle feed is certified organic. That means that no chemical fertilizers or **pesticides** can be used on the grazing pastures. In addition, organic cows must have constant access to outdoor grazing land. Many farmers cannot meet all of the requirements. While the meat from their farms may be natural and sustainable, it cannot be labeled organic.

These cows are being raised sustainably.

Grass fed in Brazil

Brazil is the world's largest beef exporter. There are about 200 million beef cows in Brazil. These cows spend their days grazing in pasturelands. Unlike cows in the United States, they are not kept on feedlots and fed grain and antibiotics. This is one reason why the demand for Brazilian beef is high.

Unfortunately, Brazil's dominance in the world meat market has taken a high toll on the Amazon Rain Forest. Large parts of the rain forest have been destroyed to make more room for grazing pastures. Brazil plans to double its beef production by 2018, which means that even more rain forest will be destroyed.

These cattle are grazing on land that used to be rain forest.

Life for the Maasai centers around their cattle.

Cattle as a way of life for the Maasai

The Maasai are an **indigenous** people living in Kenya and Tanzania. In many ways, the life of the Maasai centers around their cattle. Cows are the Maasai's primary food source. They not only drink cow milk and eat cow meat, they also occasionally drink cow blood. A mixture of cow blood and milk is used for rituals and given to people who are sick. The number of cows a man owns defines both his wealth and his status. The Maasai are a **nomadic** people, traveling with their herds to find water and grazing land.

The Maasai believe that cattle were created by their god specifically for their use. The Maasai have lost much of their land to the Kenyan government, which has used the land to create wildlife preserves. They have also suffered huge losses from **droughts**, which have become more common in recent years.

How Is Poultry Farmed?

Although chicken is the most popular kind of **poultry**, people also eat turkey, duck, ostrich, partridge, and a variety of other birds. Chickens raised for meat are called **broilers**. In the past, most of the world's chickens were raised in people's yards for family consumption and perhaps to sell at the local market. Today nearly three-fourths of all broilers worldwide are raised in huge chicken houses on **CAFOs**. The United States produces more poultry than any other country. China and Brazil also produce large amounts of poultry.

Cecile Steele

Cecile Steele is often called the mother of the modern poultry industry. She was the first to farm large numbers of broilers. When the poultry company accidently sent 500 chicks instead of 50 to her Delaware farm in 1923, rather than sending them back she took on the challenge of raising them all. She found her new business so profitable that within five years she and her husband were raising 27,000 chickens at a time.

Plenty of poultry

In the United States, broilers are hatched in large **incubators**. Thousands of chickens live in crowded, windowless chicken houses. During their six to eight weeks of life, they eat feed that has been engineered for maximum growth. The feed also includes **antibiotics** to fight diseases that are caused by the **unsanitary** conditions. Many people feel it is **unethical** to raise chickens under these conditions. Countries in Europe have different, and often higher, standards for raising poultry.

These chickens will spend their entire lives in a dark, crowded chicken house.

These chickens are being raised naturally instead of in CAFOs.

Free-range chickens

In most of the world, the term "free range" means that the chickens spend a good portion of their lives in large outdoor pastures roaming free and eating grass. However, in the United States the term "free range" simply means that the chickens have access to the outdoors. That may mean that there is a small door on one end of a huge chicken house that leads to a dirt or gravel yard. Under these circumstances few of the chickens actually spend any time outdoors, and yet they can still be labeled free range.

Some farmers choose to raise smaller flocks than those in CAFOs. They also may choose not to use antibiotics and other chemicals, preferring to raise their chickens more naturally. Raising true free-range chickens is more expensive than raising chickens in giant chicken houses. Often consumers do not want to pay the difference.

Backyard Chicken Coop

People who want to keep a few chickens need to have a small coop. There are many different designs for backyard coops. Some even look like miniature barns or houses.

Backyard chickens

Many families in suburban and even urban neighborhoods raise small flocks of chickens. Some people allow their chickens to have access to their entire yards, while others build a smaller fenced-in area, not only to keep their chickens in one place, but also to keep them safe from predators.

Chickens in developing countries

Owning a small flock of chickens can make a huge difference for poor families in **developing countries** in Africa, South America, and Asia. Not only do the chickens supply these families with eggs and meat, but they can also be bred, and the chicks can be sold. In some countries in Africa, women have very little education and few opportunities to make money. Raising chickens allows these women to provide for their families.

Migratory duck farming in India

In Kerala, India, duck farmers have found a way to feed their flocks while helping local farmers. After the rice harvest, large flocks of ducks are released into **rice paddies** to eat what is left. Their droppings **fertilize** the soil for the next rice crop.

Chance Christine: Ugandan Chicken Farmer

Raising chickens has changed Chance Christine's life. Before she began raising her flock, she was selling porridge by the roadside and was not making enough to feed and clothe her three children. Now her children are clothed, well fed, and attending school.

Each year farmers split their flocks into groups of 500 birds and hire farm laborers to take the ducks on a four-month journey across hundreds of rice fields to the neighboring state of Tamil Nadu. The ducks eat rice, slugs, and insects in the fields along the way. The rice farmers are given eggs for letting the ducks search for food in their paddies. In Tamil Nadu, mature ducks are sold for their meat, and the rest are trucked back home.

These ducks are eating what
is left after the rice harvest.

How Are Pigs and Sheep Farmed?

Pork is one of the most widely eaten meats in the world. Pig products include pork as well as ham and bacon. Most pigs in the United States are raised on huge **CAFOs**. A single CAFO may contain more than 10,000 hogs at a time.

These pigs are being raised in crowded CAFOs.

One of the biggest concerns with large pig farms is the huge amounts of manure that the pigs produce. One hog secretes about 6 pounds (2.7 kilograms) of manure each day. The manure is drained into football-field-sized cesspools called lagoons. The smell from these lagoons is overpowering and travels for miles. Further, the manure releases toxic fumes that have caused serious health problems in children and the elderly.

China's swine

China produces the most pork by far compared to any other country. Nearly half of all the world's pigs are located in China. Almost all of the pigs in China are raised for domestic consumption. Pig farming in China is **subsidized** by the government. This means that the government gives pig farmers money that they can then spend on housing, feed, and other expenses. Issues of food safety are not unusual in China's pork industry. Farms have been shut down for **unsanitary** conditions and use of illegal drugs.

Smithfield Foods

Smithfield Foods is the world's largest producer of pork. The company is based in Smithfield, Virginia, but has farms and processing plants in 26 states as well as in several countries, including China, Brazil, Mexico, and the United Kingdom.

Pigs in Denmark

Denmark is one of the most successful pig-raising countries and is the world's largest exporter of pork products. It exports 85 percent of its pork to 130 different countries.

Denmark has enacted a set of animal welfare laws that have improved the lives of their pigs. These include treatment of mother sows and piglets, living conditions, and transport of the animals. These laws have helped to keep their pigs healthy and the meat they produce safe. In addition, scientists in Denmark are working to reduce the odor from swine waste.

Adopt a pig in Nova Scotia

Maple Lane Farms is a family-owned farm in Nova Scotia, Canada. In the mid-2000s, Maple Lane Farms was losing money due to rising feed costs and low pork prices. It was costing more to raise their pigs than they could get from the meat packers who bought them. The family was nearing **bankruptcy** when they decided to try an "Adopt-a-Pig" program.

They soon found that customers were eager to join the program. To adopt a pig, the customer paid up front, while the pig was still young, and the customer paid more for a pig than the farmers got from the meat packers. However, for that extra money the customer would get meat from a pig that was raised naturally on a farm instead of on a CAFO. After slaughter, the pig was cut and wrapped to the customer's specification and delivered at no extra cost. There are similar programs on other farms.

Piglets raised on farms outdoors are healthier than those raised in giant CAFOs.

In Australia, sheep are raised on large ranches called stations.

Sheep Down Under

Australia and New Zealand are the world's top sheep producers. Sheep are raised on large ranches called **stations**. Often sheep and cows are raised together on one station. Sheep graze freely on the land until they are ready for slaughter. In Australia a station may be so large that it takes days to round up all of the sheep. Well-trained sheep dogs help to herd the sheep. On very large stations, low-flying helicopters may also be used. In New Zealand there are 11 times more sheep than people!

Most people prefer lamb, which means the animal must be slaughtered before it is a year old. Older sheep meat is called mutton. Mutton tends to be tougher and have a stronger flavor.

Sheep Dogs

Sheep dogs in Australia have been used on large stations for hundreds of years and are still an important part of station life today. They are intelligent, tough, and able to work in hot weather. Sheep dogs herd sheep, round up strays, and keep predators away from the herd.

Bringing back mutton

Mutton was once a popular choice; however, today most people prefer lamb. Meat producers like this trend because it means that they can save money on feed and housing by slaughtering their animals earlier. However, some farmers are bucking this trend. Rather than slaughtering lambs, some farms sell older sheep. They feel that this practice is more **humane** as it allows the sheep to live into adulthood.

What Other Kinds of Meat Are Farmed?

People in different parts of the world eat all kinds of meat. Some of these meats are hunted and some are raised on farms. Meat raised on farms includes ostrich, alligator, emu, guinea pig, turtle, and frog. In most cases these kinds of animals are raised on small farms, not large **CAFOs**. Oftentimes farming animals that are found in the wild keeps people from hunting them. Meats that are not commonly eaten are sometimes called exotic meats.

Eating alligators

Alligators are a part of traditional southern Cajun cuisine (food). It is illegal to hunt alligators in the United States, so people who enjoy alligator meat must purchase it from farms. Alligator farms in the southern United States often also operate as tourist attractions. Visitors can see some of the alligators in special viewing areas.

Raising alligators is not easy. Alligator farmers must follow strict regulations and keep careful records of every alligator they raise. An alligator egg takes about 60 days to hatch. After hatching, the babies live in rearing tanks for a few months. When they are about 2 feet (0.6 meter) long, they are moved to grow houses. In order to grow large fast, alligators must be kept in a hot environment—around 90°F (32°C)—and frequently fed meat-based meal. Once an alligator is 5 to 7 feet (1.5 to 2 meters) long it is ready to be slaughtered for meat, hide, and teeth.

These alligators are being farmed for their meat, hides (skins), and teeth.

Guinea pigs for dinner

Guinea pigs are part of the cuisine in Peru and other Latin American countries. In Peru about 65 million guinea pigs are eaten every year. Guinea pig meat can be found in restaurants, fresh or frozen in the store, or even live in the markets.

Raising guinea pigs is not difficult or expensive. Rather than eating expensive feed, guinea pigs can live on alfalfa, corn husks, and table scraps. Guinea pigs have been bred to grow big and fat—up to 7 pounds (3.2 kilograms)! Peruvian women who were previously living in **poverty** are now making money raising guinea pigs. Guinea pig meat is also being exported to the United States, Japan, and several European countries.

These guinea pigs aren't pets. They are being raised to be eaten.

These emus are being raised for their meat on a farm in Australia.

Emu farms in Australia

An emu is a large, flightless bird native to Australia. **Aboriginal people** have been eating emus for thousands of years. Today emus in the wild are a protected species, so only emus raised on farms may be eaten.

Emus are raised on farms in every Australian state. There are about 250 emu farms in Australia. Emus are raised in large, open-air pens and fed grain to supplement the leaves and grass they eat during the day. A full-grown emu is about six-and-a-half feet tall (2 meters). It takes about 14 months to raise an emu for slaughter. Emu farms are environmentally friendly because farmers do not need to clear any land to raise emus, and their soft feet do not destroy the land.

What Are the Negative Aspects of the Meat Industry?

There are more people in the world than ever before, and many of them like to eat meat. It takes a great deal of land, energy, and other resources to raise enough animals to meet the world's demand. **CAFOs** are able to raise large numbers of animals cheaply. However, many agree that raising animals on large factory farms is cruel to the animals, unhealthy for the humans who consume them, and harmful to the planet.

Animal ethics

Animals raised on large CAFOs are crowded together in large, windowless, warehouse-like buildings. The animals have little room to move and are often forced to live in their own waste. Crowded, **unsanitary** conditions make for many sick animals. Ten percent of animals in CAFOs die from stress or disease before they are old enough for slaughter. Many people feel it is **unethical** to treat animals this way and refuse to eat meat that comes from CAFOs.

Dr. Temple Grandin

Temple Grandin was born in 1947 with **autism**. She believes that her autism gives insight about how animals think and feel. Unlike most people, Grandin thinks in pictures instead of words. Grandin has dedicated her life to creating more **humane** ways to keep, transport, and slaughter animals. Today nearly half the cattle in the United States and Canada are processed in facilities that were designed by Grandin. Grandin has written several important books about autism and animal behavior. In 2010 HBO made an award-winning movie about her life starring Claire Danes.

Dr. Temple Grandin helps farmers to treat their animals more humanely.

Unhealthy for people

Many people have become sick and even died from eating tainted meat or working with sick animals. Some of the more serious illnesses include: salmonella, E. coli, Creutzfeldt-Jakob disease (CJD), swine flu, and avian flu. In addition, the **antibiotics** and **growth hormones** that are given to animals in CAFOs can cause other serious health problems, such as cancer. This is why these practices have been banned in Europe. Further, working on a ranch or in a slaughterhouse is extremely dangerous. Many workers have been injured or even killed on the job.

These chickens have all died because of unsanitary conditions and cannot be eaten.

This lagoon is covered with a sheet to trap gases released by pig waste.

Environmental issues

Large amounts of land are needed to graze cattle and to grow grain to feed cattle and other animals that are raised for meat. Nearly one-third of the world's landmass is used for raising **livestock**. Often, rain forests are cleared to create this land. Rain forests help to prevent **global warming** by absorbing carbon dioxide in the air.

Meat production contributes to global warming in other ways, too. Worldwide, the meat industry accounts for 18 percent of the planet's **greenhouse gas** emissions. That is more than all of the world's cars, boats, planes, and trains combined, which only contribute 13 percent. Part of these emissions is in the form of **nitrous oxide**, which comes from the manure these animals produce. Another part comes from the **methane gas** that cows release in large amounts every day. More emissions are created by the transportation of feed for the animals to eat, transportation to the slaughterhouses, and transportation of the meat products themselves to stores and restaurants.

What Is the Future of Farming Meat?

Many factors will affect how the **livestock** industry grows. As the world's population increases, demand for meat will also increase. However, resources such as energy, land, and water are becoming scarcer. While many more people are eating meat than ever before, **vegetarianism** is also a growing trend. People may stop eating meat to improve their own health or the health of the planet, or because they do not want to contribute to the **unethical** treatment of animals.

Stricter regulations

The future is also likely to bring stricter regulations about how **CAFO** operators treat their animals and manage waste. Routine use of **antibiotics** in livestock has been banned in Europe, as well as the use of **growth hormones** for cattle. Similar bans may be coming to the United States. Improvements in the meat industry are likely to come at a price. Consumers will have to pay more for the meat that they buy.

Sustainable farming

With more people demanding ethical treatment of animals and better management of the land, **sustainable farms** are on the rise. Small farmers continue to find ways to raise animals with minimal environmental impact. Raising livestock in a natural way costs considerably more than raising them on factory farms. However, many people are willing to pay more money for meat that they know was raised ethically without hormones and antibiotics.

These cows are eating feed that has been ground and mixed right on the farm.

Grain Grinder and Mixer

While large CAFOs buy premixed grain, some small farms grind and mix their own grains in machines to make the perfect food for their animals.

More meat for developing countries

As **developing countries** get richer, their meat consumption increases. Many families that were once too poor to afford much meat now find that they have enough money to have meat with every meal.

Smaller farms are helping to fill this demand for more meat. Many groups are helping poor people to start raising livestock by giving them small loans to buy livestock and educating them on how to care for their animals. New technologies, such as improving the quality of foraging grasses, are being created specifically for these small farmers.

Dr. Athol Klieve: Research Scientist

Australian scientist Dr. Athol Klieve believes that kangaroos may be able to help reduce the amount of methane released by cattle. Both cattle and kangaroos have **bacteria** in their guts that help to break down the food that they eat. This process produces methane in cows, but in kangaroos it produces acetate—a substance similar to vinegar. Klieve wants to replace the methane-producing bacteria in cows with the acetate-producing bacteria in kangaroos. This would not only reduce methane gas, but would also give the cows more energy!

Dr. Athol Klieve is working to reduce the amount of methane gas released by cows.

Climate change will affect farmers all over the world, including this shepherdess in Tibet.

Climate change

Global warming will affect meat farmers all over the world. As the planet gets warmer, there will be changes in the way that livestock feed is grown. It is possible that there will even be feed shortages. There are also likely to be stricter regulations to prevent livestock's contribution to global warming. Restrictions on how much land can be cleared and regulations about emissions from waste and animals are likely to be enacted.

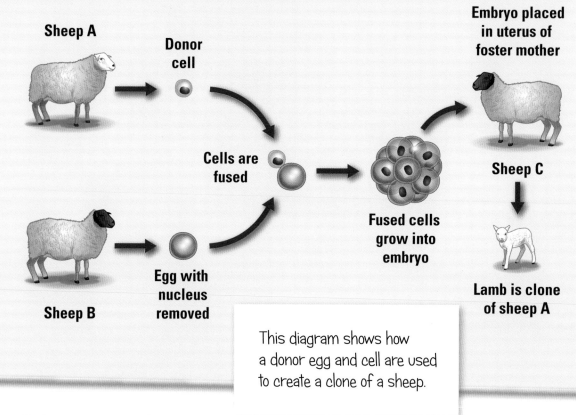

Sheep A

Donor cell

Cells are fused

Sheep B

Egg with nucleus removed

Fused cells grow into embryo

Embryo placed in uterus of foster mother

Sheep C

Lamb is clone of sheep A

This diagram shows how a donor egg and cell are used to create a clone of a sheep.

Science on the farm

Agricultural scientists are working to find more technologies to improve meat production. Although some of these are aimed at raising the quality of life for the animals, most are focused on finding ways to grow bigger animals in a shorter amount of time.

Genetics

Genetics and breeding have already played a huge part in the industry and will continue to do so in the future. Because of **selective breeding**, the animals we eat today are much bigger than those that were eaten a hundred years ago. In the future, scientists may manipulate animal **DNA** with **genetic engineering** to produce animals that grow faster and bigger.

Cloning

Cloning is the process of making a duplicate or identical twin of an animal using the animal's DNA. This is achieved by fusing DNA from an adult animal with an egg that has had the **nucleus** removed, and then implanting the egg into an adult animal's uterus to grow. In the future, cloning could be used to duplicate the best animals on a farm many times in order to improve the stock.

In vitro meat

In vitro meat is animal flesh that has never been a part of a whole, living animal. In vitro meat is grown in labs by taking muscle cells from animals and adding protein to make them grow. Scientists working on in vitro meat hope that the process will become a safer, less expensive, and more **humane** way to produce large amounts of meat.

Dolly the sheep was the first mammal ever to be cloned.

How Important Is the Meat Industry?

Meat is a large and important industry. All over the world, billions of animals are being raised for meat. Over a billion humans are working to get these animals raised, slaughtered, and onto your plate.

CAFO operators and farmers spend their lives managing these animals. Other farmers raise grain to feed these animals. Still more people transport the grain to farms and CAFOs and, when they are ready, transport the animals to the slaughterhouses.

At the slaughterhouses, workers process the animals and pack the meat. Then even more people are needed to transport the meat to stores and restaurants. In addition, there are people who make the tools and equipment needed to raise and process animals, scientists and researchers who work to improve the industry, and inspectors whose job is to make sure that everyone is following meat industry regulations.

Because the demand for meat is so high, the meat industry faces many challenges. For most of the meat we eat, the welfare of the animals isn't always the highest priority to the farmers. In addition, the meat industry is taking a heavy toll on the planet in terms of pollution, global warming, and loss of rain forest.

Eating meat raised on **sustainable farms** is one way to help our planet. Even though sustainable meat is more expensive than factory-farmed meat, many people feel that contented animals and a healthy planet are worth the price.

These cows are being raised on a sustainable farm for a healthier planet.

Glossary

aboriginal people people native to Australia

antibiotic drug that cures or prevents illnesses and infections caused by bacteria

autism mental disorder marked by difficulty in communication and social interactions

bacteria tiny, one-celled organisms; germs

bankruptcy not having enough money

botanist person who studies plants

broiler chicken raised for meat

bubonic plague epidemic disease that killed half of the population of Europe in the Middle Ages

cloning process of creating an animal or plant that is an exact copy of another animal or plant

composting using decaying vegetation and manure for fertilizer

concentrated animal feeding operation (CAFO) factory farm used for raising large numbers of animals in relatively small spaces, usually indoors

developing country poor country that is in the process of becoming more advanced economically

DNA genetic information found in the nucleus of a cell

domesticate to train an animal to live with or work for humans

drought long period without enough rainfall

feedlot area or building where animals are fattened for slaughter

fertilizer substance added to soil to promote plant growth

feudal system system of land ownership and labor in Europe in the Middle Ages

genetic engineering scientific process of changing a plant or animal by combining pieces of genetic material (DNA) from different species.

global warming gradual increase of the planet's temperature caused by increasing amounts of pollution

greenhouse gas gas that contributes to global warming by absorbing radiation

growth hormone substance that regulates the growth of plants or animals

humane compassion or sympathy for animals or humans

incubator equipment used for keeping eggs warm until they hatch

indigenous living in a place for a very long time

livestock animals kept on a farm

methane gas colorless, odorless gas that contributes to global warming

nitrous oxide colorless gas that contributes to global warming

nomadic moving frequently from place to place

nucleus central part of a cell that contains genetic information

organic raised naturally without the use of synthetic chemicals

pesticide chemical used for killing insects or other pests, especially on plants

poultry domestic birds raised for their meat or eggs

poverty when a person does not have enough money for food, shelter, and basic needs

rice paddy flooded field where rice is grown

station large ranch in Australia or New Zealand

selective breeding intentionally producing animals or plants with desired traits

subsidized to give financial support

sustainable farm farm that uses methods that do not harm the environment

temperament general way in which a person or animal reacts and behaves

trait specific quality

unethical morally wrong

unsanitary dirty and unhealthy—likely to cause disease

vegetarianism diet that does not include any meat

Find Out More

Books

Bailey, Gerry. *Farming for the Future*. New York: Gareth Stevens, 2011.

Buller, Laura. *Food*. New York: DK Publishing, 2005.

Craats, Rennay. *Maasai*. New York: Weigl, 2005.

Harmon, Daniel E. *Fish, Meat, and Poultry: Dangers in the Food Supply*. New York: Rosen Central, 2008.

Roth, Ruby. *That's Why We Don't Eat Animals*. Berkeley, Calif.: North Atlantic Books, 2009.

Simmons, Mark. *Teddy's Cattle Drive: A Story from History*. Albuquerque, N.M.: University of New Mexico Press, 2005.

Vogel, Julia. *Local Farms and Sustainable Foods*. Ann Arbor, Mich.: Cherry Lake, 2010.

Websites

Farm Animals
This website has pictures and information about farm animals in Kansas.

www.cyberspaceag.com/farmanimals/default.htm

Factory Farms
Learn about the dark side of factory farms and about sustainable farming from this site that includes a video talk from an informed eleven year old.

http://tiki.oneworld.net/food/food3.html

Organic Consumers Association (OCA)
This is the website of the Organic Consumers Association (OCA), which operates in the United States and Canada. The site explains the aims of the OCA and provides information and news on organic farmers and farming practices. You can read reports of the latest OCA campaigns and find a list of organic events for each state.

www.organicconsumers.org/

USDA Farm Service Agency

Learn about young farmers, fun farm facts, and more on this farming website of the USDA Farm Service Agency just for kids!

www.fsa.usda.gov/FSA/kidsapp?area=home&subject=landing&topic=landing

Places to visit

Cattle Raisers Museum

1600 Gendy Street
Fort Worth, TX 76107
817-332-8551
The Cattle Raisers Museum is located inside the Fort Worth Museum of Science and History and deals with the history of cattle raising and ranching in Texas.

www.cattleraisersmuseum.org/index.html

The Farmers' Museum

5775 State Highway 80
Cooperstown, NY 13326
607-547-1450
The Farmers' Museum in New York state is one of the oldest rural (country) life museums in the United States.

www.farmersmuseum.org

Gatorama: Alligator and Crocodile Adventure

6180 US Hwy 27
Palmdale, FL 33944
863-675-0623
You can see live alligators at Gatorama, but you can also buy alligator meat, if you're curious what it tastes like.

http://gatorama.com

Index